AFFIRMING C

Anthony E. Harvey

MARRIAGE, DIVORCE AND THE CHURCH

Series Editor: Jeffrey John

DARTON·LONGMAN+TODD

First published in 1997 by
Darton, Longman and Todd Ltd
1 Spencer Court
140–142 Wandsworth High Street
London SW18 4JJ

in association with

Affirming Catholicism
St Giles Church
No 4, The Postern
Wood Street, The Barbican
London EC2Y 8BJ

ISBN 0–232–52224–3

Designed by Bet Ayer
Phototypeset by Intype London Ltd
Printed and bound in Great Britain by
Page Bros, Norwich

Affirming Catholicism

Affirming Catholicism is a movement (not an ecclesiastical party) which exists to do two things. We affirm our confidence in our Anglican heritage; and we seek to renew and promote the Catholic tradition within it. Our aim is to explore, explain and share with others both inside and outside the Church a lively, intelligent and inclusive Catholic faith. In the words of our Trust Deed:

> It is the conviction of many that a respect for scholarship and free enquiry has been characteristic of the Church of England and of the Churches of the wider Anglican Communion from earliest times, and is fully consistent with the status of those Churches as part of the Holy Catholic Church. It is desired to establish a charitable educational foundation which will be true both to those characteristics and to the Catholic tradition within Anglicanism ... The object of the foundation shall be the advancement of education in the doctrines and the historical development of the Church of England and the Churches of the wider Anglican Communion, as held by those standing within the Catholic tradition.

Our Publications

These are offered as one means of presenting Anglican Catholic teaching and practice in as clear and accessible a form as possible. Some cover traditional doctrinal and liturgical themes; others attempt to present a well-argued Catholic viewpoint on issues of debate currently facing the Church. There is a list of our series of booklets on page v.

The present series of books is provided, where appropriate, with summaries to sections, and suggested questions which we hope will facilitate personal study or discussion in groups. Other titles in the present series are:

> *Is There an Anglican Way? – Scripture, Church and Reason: New Approaches to an Old Triad* Ross Thompson
> *The Ministry of Deliverance* Dominic Walker OGS
> *By What Authority? – Authority, Ministry and the Catholic Church* Mark D. Chapman

To order these publications individually or on subscription, or for further information about the aims and activities of Affirming Catholicism, write to:

> The Secretary
> Affirming Catholicism
> St Giles Church
> No 4, The Postern
> Wood St
> Barbican
> London EC2Y 8BJ
>
> Tel 0171 638 1980
> Fax 0171 638 1997

Booklets in the Affirming Catholicism series

———

About the Author

Anthony Harvey is a former Lecturer in Theology, Fellow of Wolfson College and Chaplain of the Queen's College, Oxford. In 1982 he became Canon of Westminster and Sub-Dean in 1987. He served on the Doctrine Commission of the Church of England and the Archbishop's Commission on Urban Priority Areas.

His publications include *Strenuous Commands: The Ethic of Jesus* and *Promise or Pretence: A Christian's Guide to Sexual Morals*.

Contents

MARRIAGE, DIVORCE AND THE CHURCH

Marriage: the Institution?

In any discussion of marriage it is essential to remember that we are speaking not of a religious institution but of a <u>social one</u>. Religions, for good reason, have a significant interest in marriage, and may make an important contribution to the understanding and regulation of it. But marriage existed before any of the world's great religions was born, and has assumed a great variety of forms both within and outside the spheres of influence of those religions.

Marriage is entered upon for a variety of reasons: to secure a family inheritance or a personal fortune, to cement a political or dynastic alliance, to give status and security to an alien, to form a partnership based on romantic love. It performs a vital role in the ordering and stability of society and in the nurturing of children; and because it involves the transmission of a family name and property, and affects the civil status of both men and women, it is entered upon for life and is never seen as an arrangement which can be terminated by the parties at will. The interests of others are involved, and one of the spouses may stand to lose money, property and status as a result of separation. Divorce therefore is regulated, and may be contested, by due process of law.

The interest of a religion in this institution normally begins with the conviction that marriage is more than a matter of social convenience and personal choice: it was 'ordained by God', and flows from the very nature of human beings, a natural consequence of their creation as male and female (Gen. 2:24). This apparent divine endorsement of the institution may be interpreted (as in the Jewish tradition) as an obligation laid on every male to contract a marriage and have offspring – a view tempered in Christianity by the honour paid to celibacy, which was the result of one interpretation (not the only possible one) of Jesus' saying about 'eunuchs for the sake of the kingdom', and of St Paul's insistence on the importance of being so far as possible unencumbered by domestic preoccupations in view of (as he believed) the imminent end of the present world order. A religion might also claim authority to regulate the choice of a marriage partner, whether to reinforce a social ban on incest and intermarriage (the 'forbidden degrees', Lev. 18) or to maintain the purity of the religious community (Ezra 9–10; 1 Cor. 7:12–16; 2 Cor. 6:14). But the main focus of religious attention is on strengthening the marriage tie and the family relationships which flow from it. This is done by exerting moral pressure on the spouses to fulfil their obligations to one another and those dependent on them and, where possible and appropriate, by insisting on rigorous conditions to be fulfilled in the event of divorce.

Jesus and Divorce

In Jewish society in the time of Jesus, as in the Greco-Roman world, divorce was readily available, though the legal determination of property rights could make it financially unattractive: unless the wife could be proved to be seriously at fault the husband would be liable to pay back the original dowry. (There was no direct means, as there was in the Graeco-Roman world, for a wife to divorce her husband.) The question whether or not a man was allowed to divorce his wife without repayment depended on the interpretation of the word 'disgrace' in Moses' teaching about divorce in Deuteronomy 24:1. According to some (the followers of Shammai) the disgrace must mean <u>sexual misconduct on the wife's part.</u> Others (the followers of Hillel) interpreted it much more widely to mean <u>various kinds of domestic inadequacy</u>. This debate is the context of the question with which Jesus was 'tested' according to Mark 10:2 (Matthew 19:3) and to which he gave his own answer. Discouragement from resorting to divorce arose more from the moral tradition than from legal restraints: the prophet Malachi invoked divine disapproval on divorce, especially when it was a case of a man deserting a wife after years of marriage in order to marry a younger woman (Mal. 2:14–16); and the Wisdom tradition, basing itself on the value of partnership in marriage (Gen. 2:18; Tobit 8:6), stressed the advantage of permanent marriage with a good wife, while conceding that some women could become intolerable wives to an extent that justified divorce (Eccles. 25:26). Before Jesus, we know of no moral teacher who expressed himself utterly opposed to divorce. In this respect the contribution of Jesus is unprecedented and distinctive: his disapproval of divorce was clear and unequivocal. In his view divorce was, quite simply, wrong.

But it is one thing to say that divorce is morally wrong. It is quite another thing to infer from this that there are no circumstances whatever under which it might be allowable; or even (an inference that came to be drawn later on) that divorce is in some sense impossible. And there is a further problem: if Jesus founded a community that was to be guided by his teaching, how was this community, set amidst a society in which divorce was well established and regulated by law, to embody in the lives of its members that definitive renunciation of divorce which seemed to be implied by Jesus' recorded words? On all these questions the evidence of Scripture is tantalizingly ambivalent, and no two historic Churches have drawn precisely the same conclusions or adopted precisely the same policies.

Let us begin with the first of these questions: was Jesus' disapproval of divorce *unconditional*? On this, the evidence of the Gospels is notoriously difficult to handle. In Mark and Luke divorce followed by remarriage is said to be equivalent to adultery, meaning as serious as a capital offence. This reads like a blanket condemnation. But in Matthew there is an exception: the case of *porneia*, or sexual unfaithfulness. This makes the saying into a rule that applies to most, but not all, circumstances. Which did Jesus intend, an absolute prohibition or a rule admitting of exceptions?

For most of the history of the Church, this question was answered more or less *a priori*. It was accepted by all that both forms of the prohibition were spoken by Jesus. Those who assumed that adultery must necessarily be a valid ground for divorce took the formulation in Matthew to represent Jesus' meaning, that in Mark and Luke being simply a terse abbreviation of it (this was the dominant patristic view). Those whom today we might call 'rigorists' did not deny that Jesus (according to Matthew) allowed for the possibility of divorce in certain cases, but stressed that this was a concession to 'hardness of heart': no Christian should take advantage of it, but should follow the stricter teaching according to Mark and Luke.

Modern biblical scholarship has now set the discussion on a different path. It is no longer required to believe that both formulations go back to Jesus. Either the 'original' form is the rigorous and comprehensive prohibition found in Mark and Luke, the 'Matthaean exception' being a later adjustment to accommodate the teaching to the realities of church life; or the Matthaean form is the earliest, correctly locating Jesus' teaching within legal discussions known to have been in progress at the time, but subsequently stripped of its technical legal character and reported as a general moral prohibition in the less 'Jewish' environments represented by Mark and Luke. Neither solution appears capable of decisive proof. The view taken by interpreters is still liable to depend on prior assumptions. That Jesus was against divorce is incontestable. But any attempt to say more than this and to derive rules or principles from his teaching runs into difficulties created by the ambiguity of the evidence.

It is however possible to approach the question from a different direction. From what we know of Jesus, can we say anything about the *kind* of teaching he was likely to give? Was he legislating – that is, proposing a reform of the Law of Moses? Was he propounding a code that should govern the life of his followers? Was he simply making a moral judgment? All these approaches have had their advocates. It has been argued, for instance, that the story of the Transfiguration represents Jesus as inheriting the role of both Moses and Elijah – the law-giver as well as the prophet; that Matthew's Gospel deliberately emphasizes his legislative activity, placing his 'Sermon' on the 'Mount' – a new Sinai – and giving Jesus an authority explicitly superior to that of Moses ('it was said ... but I say'); and that it was part of his mission to repeal the 'concession' made by Moses in the matter of divorce.

It has to be said, though, that this interpretation of Matthew's Gospel, popular as it was some years ago, has been increasingly called into question, and in any case is not easy to fit into the realities of the legal situation as it existed in the time of Jesus. For most purposes – and certainly in matters of domestic and family law – the inhabitants of Palestine lived under the biblical Law of Moses, which was administered in local courts composed of semi-professional judges well versed in Scripture and its interpretation. The application of particular laws to the case in hand was often a matter of dispute; there were different schools of thought among 'doctors of the law', and we read of Jesus being drawn into their arguments. But to seek to change or reform the law itself would have seemed, first, blasphemous: the Law was given by God, and to question its eternal validity was to strike at the heart of Jewish identity – when this charge was laid against Paul it was regarded as very serious indeed (Acts 18:13; 21:28); secondly, it could have had little effect: there was no way in which a radical revision of the law itself could have rapidly replaced the legal tradition within which lawyers had been working for generations. To represent Jesus as a 'new Moses', propounding a revised version of the Torah, is to fly in the face of historical probabilities.

More plausible, at first sight, is the suggestion that Jesus was laying down a code of conduct that was intended to have the force of law, not for the entire Jewish people, but for the community of his followers. There is ample precedent for this. The Qumran 'Manual of Discipline' contains regulations that were to be observed by the members of that particular Jewish sect; and a number of other groups are known to have existed which evolved their own mode of law-abiding life and demanded from their members obedience to a particular discipline. But in all these cases one factor is constant: the rules by which the sect proposed to live had definite sanctions attached to them. Transgressions carried stated penalties, and anyone who consistently refused to conform would be excluded from the community.

It is true that there are traces of such disciplinary procedures in Matthew's Gospel; but it has to be said that the general thrust of Jesus' teaching moves in a quite different direction. Far from laying down rules that his followers must keep, or else risk exclusion, Jesus appears to have challenged his hearers to a free response, to have taught by particular (sometimes extreme) instances rather than systematic codes of conduct, and to have stressed the potential for relationships with God and one's neighbour of repentance, forgiveness and reconciliation. To cast him in the role of the founder and legislator of a sect is to do violence to a mass of Gospel evidence; indeed it is not even certain that he envisaged an enduring community of followers at all.

We are left with the third possibility: Jesus was neither a legislator nor the disciplinarian authority for a sect but a teacher whose purpose was to improve the moral quality of people's lives. As such, he stood in a long and respected tradition, both of the prophets (much of whose teaching was similarly concerned with moral conduct) and of 'wisdom' teachers whose prudential approach to morality gave international currency to their maxims and whose activity was still an important factor in moral education. Certainly

Jesus was no ordinary moralist. His teaching had an edge, an appeal and a challenge to which it is hard to find any parallel. But his techniques – the use of parables, of *a fortiori* arguments, of exaggeration and paradox – derived from his inheritance.

One of these in particular is relevant to our question. Moral teaching for the most part is given either in the form of a maxim ('A wise son makes a glad father', Prov. 10:1) or an exhortation ('Hearken to your father who begot you', Prov. 23:22). Legislation, by contrast, typically uses a casuistic form to define cases: 'Whoever does x will receive the penalty y' ('Whosoever strikes his father or mother will be put to death', Ex. 21:15). But occasionally the distinction may be ignored. For particular emphasis the lawgiver may address the subject: 'Thou shalt not steal'. For particular effect the moralist may use a legal form: 'He that talks much with a woman brings evil upon himself' (Aboth 1:5) is a famous – perhaps we should say notorious – example from the Jewish moral tradition. It sounds like law; but then we realize that no legal system could give it effect: it is a sharpened form of moral warning.

It is this device which was sometimes used by Jesus. In particular, he used it when teaching about divorce. Hence the possibility of misunderstanding: what in reality was intended as moral teaching could be mistaken for 'a new law'.

The case is clearest when the teaching appears in the Sermon on the Mount. Jesus has just used the pseudo-legal device to convey two quite startling moral injunctions.

'Anyone who is angry with his brother shall be liable to judgment.'

Matthew 5:22

'Anyone who looks at a woman lustfully ... has already committed adultery with her in his heart'.

Matthew 5:28

The form is the typical legal prescription: anyone who does x will receive y. For a moment one might think that Jesus is recommending that anger should be a criminal offence; but one soon realizes that no human court could handle such a charge (and this is made obvious by the subsequent clause, 'shall be liable to hell-fire'), and that Jesus is using the form to make a *moral* point: anger may be *as bad as* homicide; a salacious glance may be *as bad as* adultery. Then, a few verses later, we have a third instance of exactly the same form:

'Anyone who divorces his wife ... involves her in adultery.'

In the context, the force of this saying is clearly like that of the others: divorce is as bad as adultery (a capital offence: so, very bad indeed). Which is exactly what we should expect Jesus, the moral teacher, to say. Divorce is wrong. Avoid it! And this, we can assume, is also the force of the saying even when (as later in Matthew, and in Mark and Luke) it appears in other contexts. It is exactly the kind of sharp, unconditional moral teaching which is characteristic of Jesus.

The difficulty is, of course, that each time the saying

occurs in Matthew (as opposed to Mark and Luke) it is *not* unconditional: ' . . . except in the case of unchastity.' In this case it is not only the form that reads like law; the exceptive clause makes no sense unless it qualifies a law or a rule. We have seen that it would hardly have been possible for Jesus to claim to be promulgating a law; and we found it to be unlikely (though not impossible) that he was formulating a disciplinary clause for his community. However that may be, one thing seems certain: recorded in this form in Matthew, it was taken as a rule to govern the domestic lives of congregations where this Gospel was read.

The Early Church

Such a rule there was bound to be. Jesus taught that divorce was wrong. His followers had to find a way of passing on this teaching and of giving it credibility by their own marital faithfulness. But they lived in a society which accepted divorce (at least under some circumstances) as a matter of course; and their church members were no less prone to sin and failure in this area than they were in others. It was not sufficient for Jesus' followers simply to repeat Jesus' saying that divorce is wrong. They urgently needed a rule or standard rigorous enough to reflect Jesus' clear moral stance on the matter but sufficiently realistic to allow for genuine cases of hardship in the community. Their solution was: divorce is not permissible, except in the case of fornication.

Whether or not this explanation of the clause in Matthew is correct, there can be no doubt that the problem of adapting Jesus' strong moral line to the realities of Christian life was there from the beginning, just as it has been ever since. Indeed we might reasonably hope that if we could determine what solution was adopted in the earliest days of the Church we could regard it as an authoritative guide for today.

Unfortunately our evidence on this is as ambiguous as the evidence of Jesus' teaching on the matter. Certainly Paul, when advising his converts on sexual and family matters, felt able to give them a clear ruling, derived from Jesus' teaching ('not I but the Lord'), that a woman 'should not be separated' from her husband and a man should not 'release' his wife. But he goes on (and this is the first ambiguity: it is not clear whether he is still speaking for 'the Lord') to allow for the possibility that separations will take place, in which case the wife should 'remain unmarried or be reconciled to her husband'.

From this it is clear at least that Paul did not interpret 'the Lord's' teaching as an inviolable rule; there is no suggestion that separated spouses would be excluded from the community; and his advice not to remarry could be due just as much to his personal concern that Christians should be unencumbered by domestic and family ties as to any ruling he believed could be derived from Jesus. He then goes on (explicitly on his own authority, not that of Jesus) to discuss the case of marriage where one of the spouses is a non-Christian. He encourages them to stay together, but allows again for the possibility that they may separate. Whether in this case they should resort to the courts for a divorce (as might well be necessary to establish the wife's civil status and property) he does not specify.

One thing is clear from this evidence. Paul knew of Jesus' disapproval of divorce and passed it on by way of authoritative guidance for the Church. But he was also aware that there might be a case for certain exceptions, to resolve which he made recommendations based on pragmatic considerations (such as the likelihood of an unbelieving spouse being converted, or the need to follow one's Christian calling 'in peace', without a conflict of beliefs) rather than on any rule or principle. And a similar situation obtained for at least the next two centuries in the life of the Church. All were agreed that divorce was wrong; but faced with the fact of adultery committed by Church members, with the inevitable consequence of divorce, they had to address the question whether remarriage was permissible. Various arguments were used against it. In Hermas, for example (*Mand.* 4), with the author's stress on the importance of repentance, the husband is advised not to remarry in case the wife repents and returns. In Clement, remarrying after a former marriage is not regarded as sinful but is less admirable than remaining single (*Strom.* 3:12). In Origen, similarly, remarriage is not excluded but advised against on the basis of an interpretation of a saying of Jesus (*Hom. in Matth.* 14:23). At the other extreme is Athenagoras who, with a certain logic (we must admit), took Jesus' words to imply, not 'till death us do part', but 'for ever': even the death of a spouse did not make it legitimate to marry again (*Leg.* 33).

Given this wide range of views on remarriage, and the variety of reasons advanced against it in the early centuries, it is clear that at this stage there was not thought to be any particular factor in marriages contracted by believers which made divorce and remarriage either unthinkable or even invariably sinful. There was, of course, a further saying of Jesus which bore on the question: 'What God has joined together let no man put asunder' (Mark 10:9); but this was little quoted in discussions of divorce and remarriage. And no wonder, for what does it mean? What has God 'joined together'? Does this mean every marriage that ever takes place (including that large number which, in Jesus' time, ended in divorce)? Do human beings never make a mistake? Certainly the Jews believed (though our evidence for this is somewhat later than Jesus' time) that some marriages are made in heaven – just as we may say today that two people are meant for each other. But who is to say which these marriages are? No one thought it applied to every marriage, but if it applied to some, then *those* marriage partners clearly should not contemplate divorce. And it would have been characteristic of Jesus to use this perhaps somewhat exceptional case to make a general point: your marriage *might* be one of those that God has joined together and that should not end in divorce, therefore shun divorce yourself just in case! That is at least a possible meaning of Jesus' saying. But in a society, like all those in the ancient world, where marriage was what we would now call a 'secular' affair, involving a contract, an exchange of property and solemn promises but no explicitly 'religious' ceremony, it had an oracular sound and its bearing on the marriage discipline of believers was not easily discerned.

There was, of course, teaching in the New Testament of a more positive kind. This was aimed, not at divorce or even at the moment of marriage, but at the conduct of married life when the spouses are Christians. Paul's little homily in Ephesians 5 (if it be by Paul: the question is an open one among scholars) is justly famous, and has found its way, explicitly or implicitly, into virtually every marriage service which ever takes place in a church. Not only (he writes) is there a natural analogy from caring for one's own body to caring for one's wife; and not only does Christ's self-giving love for the Church offer an example to Christian husbands of the love required of them towards their wives; but the married state itself is a pointer towards the nature of Christ's love towards the Church. The love of husband and wife is seen as the very epitome of divine love – a 'great mystery' indeed.

It is important not to romanticise the passage. It concerns the conduct of Christian husbands towards their wives. There is no hint of reciprocity. Nothing is said about the wife's love of her husband; indeed the passage ends with the daunting admonishment that the wife should 'fear' her husband – a word usually rendered in a more polite form by a translation such as 'respect' or 'honour'.

But nothing can conceal the fact that this is a world away from that equality of the sexes, that equal partnership and dignity, which is now regarded as essential to any marriage and for which indeed Christian people have striven throughout this century. For the passage is part of a recital of the moral obligations which members of a family have towards one another; and these recitals – there are two other very similar ones in the New Testament – were entirely conventional, reflecting the social and domestic ethic that was taken for granted right across the ancient world.

According to this ethic, the wife's role was to be entirely subservient to her husband and to confine herself to her domestic responsibilities. Had he lived in a different era, the author of our passage might well have talked with equal eloquence about wives as about husbands, and we are surely right to adapt his teaching to the changed situation of today. As it is, he was bound by the social mores and conventions of his time. What we can learn from him is, not an unchanging pattern of domestic relationships, but the invigorating consequence of bringing our understanding of Christ's self-giving love to bear on the deep and intimate bond which binds husband and wife together in (as we now believe) a relationship of equal dignity and evenly shared responsibility.

St Augustine

That there is, in the light of this, something special about the marriage of two Christian believers seems first to have been brought to expression by St Augustine. The question which chiefly agitated the early Church Fathers was the precise force and purchase of the 'exceptive clause' in Matthew, 'except in the case of fornication'. Did this mean that, in the case of unfaithfulness by one of the spouses, the injured party was free, not only to divorce, but to remarry? Or, given St Paul's apparently total prohibition of remarriage (admittedly not on 'the Lord's' authority) did it mean that, in this one case only, divorce was permitted but *not* remarriage? If so, then it seemed necessary to suppose that there is something in a marriage itself which has such a permanent influence on the spouses that it made sense for Jesus to say that a second marriage amounts to adultery. It is in this sense that Augustine said (*De nuptiis et concupiscentia* 1.11) that there is a 'conjugal something' (*quiddam conjugale*) which continues to exist between spouses so long as both are alive, even if they have separated, such that any second union can meaningfully be called adulterous. What is this 'something'? It is important to remember that there was nothing in the Jewish tradition, and still less in Greek and Roman law and custom, to give any support to such a notion. Divorce and remarriage were taken for granted as social institutions, and even the statement in Genesis (2:24) that husband and wife become 'one flesh' was never, so far as we know, taken to imply that a close relationship subsisted between them after they had divorced. If Christians now believed (on Jesus' authority, as they understood it) that this was so, they were advancing an entirely novel view, and were required to give an intelligible reason for it.

It was Augustine, it seems, who found the key in that same chapter of Ephesians which, as we saw, is the one passage in Scripture which offers a positive and distinctively Christian account of the married state. The author of that passage sums up the matter by saying: 'This is a great *mysterion*; and I apply it to Christ and his Church.' The precise meaning of 'mystery' in this context is a matter for debate. There are grounds for thinking that it is a way of referring to what is in fact a sexual analogy (Christ is as intimate with the Church as a husband with his wife) without stating it in a form so direct that it would excite ribald comment. However that may be, it presented itself to Augustine in a quite different way. He read St Paul, not in Greek, but in Latin. And in Jerome's Latin translation he read, not 'mystery', but *sacramentum*. This word had a variety of meanings. Primarily, it meant a military oath. In Christian theology it had also come to be used for what we now mean by 'sacrament'. But it could also mean a solemn, vowed commitment. And this was the sense of the word which gave Augustine his first clue to the nature of that 'something' which takes place in marriage and can never be undone. The couple, he suggested, had made a 'solemn vow' to one another: this would remain in existence even if they subsequently separated.

It is clear that it was not just an accident of translation which led Augustine down this path. It was also a careless (as it seems to us) disregard of the context of the sentence in question. Take the passage as a whole, and it is clear that the word 'mystery' (or *sacramentum* in Latin) applies, not to human marriage, but to the relationship between Christ and his Church. However, it would be wrong to accuse Augustine of a crass misinterpretation. He had certainly pondered deeply on the passage, and come to see that the relationship between man and wife is *in some sense* an expression of the relationship between Christ and his Church. It is only in a small way, he admits, that a purely human institution (as marriage is) can effectively reproduce the divine self-giving of Christ. Yet the word *sacramentum* suggested an analogy. Just as the 'sacrament' of baptism created a relationship with God which no subsequent apostasy could render void (for the penitent can always return and be accepted; there is no need for re-baptism), might it not be the case that a marriage, being in some sense a 'sacrament', continued in force even after separation, such that it was open, for instance, to a penitent adulterer to return to a former spouse even after divorce? (Cf. *De conjugiis adulterinis* 2.5.)

Marriage as a Sacrament

It cannot be said that Augustine's thinking on this matter reached a clear conclusion. Considerable ambiguities remain. Did he think of the *sacramentum* as a solemn commitment of the spouses towards God (which would be the natural force of the analogy) or towards each other? Did he think that this 'conjugal something' subsisted between all legally married spouses or only between Christians? For we must remember that there is no evidence for any marriage ceremonies in church until at least Augustine's time, and Christians normally had what we would call a 'civil wedding' until the eleventh century: if anything made their marriage different, it was not anything done at the moment of marriage but rather, it was usually said, their 'faith'. But his use of the word 'sacrament' was to have profound consequences: according to a later understanding of the term, it was to provide what seemed a satisfactory answer to the question, answered only in terms of analogy by Augustine, what this 'conjugal something' really might be.

One reason, of course, why Augustine could not give a clearer account of the nature of this 'sacrament' was that in his time, as we have just seen, there was normally no religious ceremony of any kind at the inception of the marriage of a Christian couple. So if marriage was a 'sacrament', in what did the sacrament consist? St Paul had used the word (or rather the Greek word *mysterion*) to speak about the relationship of Christ and his Church, and to draw out the implications for the conduct of husbands and wives. But the analogy with the 'sacrament' of baptism suggested that something more than a loving or obedient mutual relationship was at stake. Not just the conduct of married life, but the fact of being married, must have a 'sacramental' character. There must be, in Augustine's phrase, a 'conjugal something' which bound the couple together.

The difficulty was that there was no single marriage institution from which one could read off the nature or essence of marriage. Different laws and customs obtained in different parts of the Roman empire – in some not even the consent of the spouses (which today is a fundamental legal requirement) was necessary for a marriage to be certified. It was not until at least the eleventh century that the Church established its right to solemnize the marriages of its members. Only then did it become possible, on the basis of what is actually said or done at the moment of marriage, to begin to work out the sense in which marriage is (in the technical sense) a 'sacrament'.

But this was by no means a simple task. There was wide disagreement on the fundamental question of what constitutes a valid marriage. The view held by the Roman authorities was that the crucial element in any marriage was the free consent of the parties. But, against this, others held that something more was necessary. Mere consent might be sufficient to validate a betrothal; a true marriage surely required a further act. In northern Europe this had, for centuries, taken the form of the 'handing over' of property (which might be deemed to include the bride herself, whether or not she had consented!) But the idea now began to gain ground that the act which decisively bound the consenting parties in marriage was their first physical intercourse. In other words, to be recognized as truly a sacrament the marriage must be consummated – an idea first formalized by Gratian in the twelfth century and still reflected in the English Law of Nullity. It was not long before the theologians found support for this in the words of Genesis, quoted by Jesus, that 'the two become one flesh' – words which had never before been interpreted in this sense.

Indissolubility

It was now, for the first time, that it seemed both possible and necessary to propound the doctrine that the marriage of two Christian persons, when certain conditions are fulfilled, becomes 'indissoluble'. In previous centuries the authorities of the Church could do no more than bring discipline to bear on the marital unions of Christians which for the most part were entered upon through secular agencies. The questions they had to decide were, for example: Should a Christian convert remain married to a pagan spouse? Should a Christian remain married to an adulterous spouse? Were there any circumstances under which the innocent party might remarry while the adulterer was still alive, or indeed at any time?

To settle these questions the evidence of Scripture was ambiguous and imprecise. The authorities of the Eastern Church, for example, took the 'Matthaean exception' to imply that remarriage after the divorce of an adulterous partner should be permitted under certain circumstances; whereas their Western counterparts, largely under the influence of Augustine, tended to regard all second marriages as impermissible while the first partner was alive. But now, with the Church increasingly in the position of being able to regulate the conditions under which a marriage could be contracted, it became possible to give more precision to the idea of marriage as a 'sacrament'. Augustine had seen an analogy between marriage and baptism: there was 'something conjugal' (which Augustine thought derived from the mutual vows and commitment of the spouses) which is as permanent as the grace given at baptism, and allows human marriage, though in a small and inferior way, to mirror the total commitment of Christ to his Church. In this sense – that of an analogy – it could be said that marriage is a sacrament. But it was now possible to take the sacramental idea considerably further. If it is by virtue of being a sacrament that a marriage can image the unbreakable union of Christ with his Church, then, as a sacrament, it must itself be unbreakable or 'indissoluble'.

In the past, the question had been whether the Church could *permit* a marriage between Christians to be dissolved and a remarriage to take place in the lifetime of both. The question now was a different one. If marriage is a sacrament, then, like other sacraments, it has consequences which cannot be rendered null and void by any human agency. Just as the grace received at baptism, though it may be neglected or forgotten at the level of consciousness, can never be lost or invalidated, so the sacramental contract of marriage creates a situation which is in some sense unalterable: it *cannot* be dissolved. But clearly this could not be true of all marriages: certain conditions must be fulfilled if a marriage was to have the sacramentality which made it a true image of Christ's indissoluble unity with its Church. These conditions could now be identified in the circumstances and form of the marriage ceremony itself – the consent of the parties, their mutual intentions, and their capacity to fulfil the obligations entered into by their contract. To these conditions was added, as we have seen, a new factor: the marriage must be physically consummated. The task of the Church was now, not to permit divorce under certain circumstances (for when marriage was understood as a sacrament this was impossible), but to determine the circumstances under which a seeming marriage might turn out not to have been a true, that is sacramental, marriage at all. So began the theory and practice of *nullity*.

We need not follow in detail the development of the Western sacramental theology of marriage over the next few centuries. But certain elements of it should be noticed. First, the alleged indissolubility of marriage is based entirely on the proposition that marriage is a sacrament and therefore effects a consequence that is irreversible. We have glanced briefly at the history of this concept and seen that its basis in Scripture is, to say the least, problematic. The word *mysterion*, when used by Paul, certainly did not mean 'sacrament' in the sense subsequently intended by the Church; and in any case he used it specifically in relation, not to human marriage, but to the union of Christ with his Church. Even the Council of Trent was forced to concede that the text of Ephesians did not prove, but only 'suggested' (*innuit*), the sacramental character of marriage.

This lack of clear authority in Scripture provided a

ready argument to the Reformers to dispute the power of Rome to determine when a marriage was or was not 'indissoluble'. Our Lord had instituted only two sacraments, Baptism and the Eucharist. The Reformers did not deny that other rites, and in particular marriage, might have some 'sacramental' character, in the sense that they had a spiritual content, and were a sign of God's gracious presence, beyond the outward form in which they were conducted. But they saw no evidence in Scripture for the marriage rite having the sacramental character and irreversible consequences ascribed to it in Roman doctrine, and in effect they reverted to the pre-scholastic practice of the Church, basing their discipline with regard to divorce and remarriage on the somewhat ambiguous teaching of Jesus as recorded in the Gospels.

Secondly, the assimilation of the Western Church's doctrine of marriage to the development of sacramental theology meant that questions had to be asked about marriage similar to those asked about other sacraments. To use the philosophical terminology of the time, what was the 'form' and the 'matter' of the sacrament? In other words, what *happened* in the marriage ceremony which gave it the force of a sacrament? It might have been expected that there would be some ecclesiastical act or ritual which would have this effect. But in fact the principle was maintained that the principal actor in the marriage ceremony is not the priest (who simply witnesses it on behalf of the Church and gives his benediction) but the couple, and the words spoken and acts performed (such as the exchange of rings) by the couple signify their free consent to the lifelong contract made between them. This, then, must be the 'matter' (the *res*) of the sacrament.

But from this a curious consequence follows. The analogy seen by Paul between marriage and the 'sacrament' of Christ's union with his Church was based, not on anything that happened when a marriage is contracted, but on the constancy and intensity of the husband's love towards his wife. By developing a 'sacramental' theology of marriage based on the moment when a marriage begins, the Church unwittingly undermined the Scriptural argument for marriage being a 'sacrament' at all, and was forced to invest with a kind of sanctity those contractual elements of the marriage rite which were inherited from secular legal institutions. It is significant that the Orthodox Churches, less concerned to elaborate a 'sacramental' doctrine of marriage, in both their marriage ceremonies and their theology stressed the mutual devotion of husband and wife and their participation in the Christian community of love and service – an emphasis which began to re-emerge in the Roman Catholic Church in the documents of Vatican II. In this they remained closer than their Western counterparts to the only basis in the New Testament for a theology of marriage – Ephesians 5.

Thirdly, the importance given since the twelfth century to the physical consummation of marriage has had a distorting influence both on doctrine and on the law of nullity. In the twelfth century it was introduced as a means of distinguishing between marriage and betrothal. If consent and contract were the basis of marriage (as existing marriage rites implied), these things were often in place before the couple actually got married. Surely something more was needed to make the marriage effectually a sacrament?

This 'something' came to be identified with sexual intercourse – it was this that 'consummated' the marriage and enabled it to be a sacrament signifying the perfect union of Christ with his Church. But the theological (and in due course legal) concentration on the point at which marriage *begins* meant that only the first act of intercourse had (from this point of view) any significance. This, again, ran counter to the thrust of the Pauline text on which the sacramental theology of marriage (and consequently its indissolubility) is based, in that Ephesians is about the marriage relationship, not about the moment when a marriage is contracted. It also had the effect of isolating the sexual act from the context of the long-term loving relationship which gives it its meaning and justification. Today, of course, it has become even more problematical, in that a large number of Christians who get married may have slept together for months if not years beforehand. But in any case the recent thinking of all the Churches on the meaning and purpose of the physical intimacy of marriage makes it impossible to think of just one act of intercourse having decisive sacramental significance.

The Church of England

At the Reformation, the Church of England decisively adopted the view of the continental reformers that Jesus had ordained only two sacraments 'necessary for salvation': even if certain other rites had a certain sacramental character, this was not such as to support a doctrine of indissolubility. Richard Hooker, for instance, makes no mention of any sacramental tie binding the spouses together other than their participation in the Eucharist (*Ecclesiastical Polity* V.18.3) and it was only a small number of divines who continued to defend absolute indissolubility.

Moreover, one of the factors in the progress of the Reformation in England was the challenge issued by the King to the Pope's authority to give or withhold a 'dispensation' from the Canon Law that regulated all matters concerning marriages and their annulment. This did not mean, of course, that for the mass of the King's subjects things were materially different. Neither civil nor ecclesiastical courts provided a remedy if couples who were granted separation by an ecclesiastical court then wished to remarry (an Act of Parliament was required for a divorce); and nullity proceedings in post-Reformation England followed the same principles (though much more restrictively) as had been laid down in the previous two centuries by the Roman authorities.

Meanwhile, the clergy of the Established Church were required by law to conduct the marriages of any couples who fulfilled the necessary conditions, such as residence in the parish and the status of the parties as single, baptized persons. Remarriage was possible only after the death of one of the spouses or when, technically, it was not a 'remarriage' at all, that is, when a court had declared a previous marriage null and void.

So things remained until the mid-nineteenth century, when the hardship caused to innocent people by adulterous spouses was at last remedied by the provision of divorce through the courts. This presented Church authorities with a new situation. How should the clergy respond to requests to be married from persons who had been legally divorced and whose former spouses were still living? The Act of 1857 allowed a clergyman to refuse to conduct such a service (though he was obliged to allow another to do so in his church building if required). Many took advantage of this exemption from the normal requirement of the law (which was to marry any persons who satisfied the legal conditions); others appealed to the 'Matthaean exception' and consented to marry the innocent party in the case of adultery. This uneasy compromise with the law of England was made still more uncomfortable by the 'Herbert' Act of 1937 which extended the grounds of divorce to include desertion, cruelty and incurable insanity. This went far beyond anything which had ever been envisaged by the Church or which could be reconciled with a literal reading of the words of Jesus as recorded in the Gospels. Only those who believed (with some plausibility, as I have argued) that Jesus was proclaiming an ideal moral standard rather than a rule of church discipline could now contemplate fulfilling their legal duty to marry such divorced persons. The rest continued to claim exemption, which was now extended to refusing the use of their churches for any such marriage.

Meanwhile, since the end of the nineteenth century, the Roman Catholic doctrine of indissolubility had begun to gain ground. This was due, at least in part, to the influence of Anglo-Catholics, though by no means all High Churchmen accepted it: Bishop King, for example, was one of those who found its pastoral implications unacceptable. It was certainly one of the reasons for a hardening of the position taken by the Lambeth Conference between 1908 and 1938; and in 1957 an Act of the Convocation of Canterbury declared that the marriage service could not be used in the case of anyone who had a former partner still living. The discipline of the Church now expressed an explicitly 'indissolubilist' view. Clergy who followed one historic interpretation of the 'Matthaean exception' and remarried the innocent party after a case of adultery – as they were legally entitled to do – would be acting in defiance of the declared doctrine of the Church of England.

This apparent consensus in favour of absolute indissolubility, which achieved its clearest formulation in the report of the Lambeth Conference of 1948 and was reaffirmed by Act of Convocation in 1957, was however short-lived. The very next Lambeth Conference of 1958, which made a notable contribution to the topic of 'The Family in Contemporary Society', recommended that the question of marriage discipline should receive further study in every province of the Anglican Communion; and in 1971 a Commission set up by the Archbishop of Canterbury on 'The Christian Doctrine of Marriage' argued that if there were 'a moral consensus' in favour of the remarriage of divorced persons this would provide a sounder basis for the Church's discipline than the theologically questionable and now pastorally problematic doctrine of indissolubility.

This argument was not generally accepted; but the acknowledged possibility of reopening the theological question, combined with the intense pressure on the clergy to minister more compassionately and effectively to the growing number of divorcees in British society, ensured that the question would not go away. There followed a series of reports and synod debates, in the course of which the discipline imposed by the Church on the clergy was considerably relaxed; and the remarriage of divorced persons, subject to certain limitations and safeguards, has now been officially authorized. In effect, the clergy of the Church of England are now free to follow their conscience; from which it can be inferred that no *doctrinal* error is being committed if a second marriage is solemnized in a church while the first partner is still alive. In the light of this it is evident that the doctrine of indissolubility has lost its short-lived hold on the teaching and practice of the Church of England.

Not that the question has been static in the Church of Rome either. Roman Catholics live in the same societies as Anglicans and come under the same pressure to recognize and adapt to the increasing prevalence of divorce. The Roman Catholic rule has remained the same, and the justification is still the 'indissoluble bond' created by the sacramental character of marriage according to the teaching of Christ and his apostle. But account has to be taken of the fact that the doctrine of indissolubility arose in a period when the Church had full control over the institution of marriage. This meant that it had the power to determine precisely what conditions must be fulfilled if a marriage were to acquire its sacramental character, and these conditions – consent, valid contract and subsequent consummation – were all ones that are still present today in the vast majority of marriages, whether or not they are solemnized in church. It becomes difficult, therefore, to see why a marriage entered upon with the rites and ceremonies of the Church thereby acquires sacramental indissolubility while a civil wedding (which contains all the same elements) does not.

Moreover, all the Churches have shown a new understanding of the physical and emotional aspects of marriage and adjusted their liturgies accordingly. No longer is intercourse seen merely as the once and for all 'consummation' of marriage, thereafter to be understood solely as the means of procreation; it is now publicly proclaimed in marriage services to lead to the constantly deepening 'union of mind and spirit' and to be a divine provision by which husband and wife may 'delight in one another'. It therefore no longer seems plausible to isolate a single act of intercourse as that which sets the seal on a marriage and ensures its sacramental indissolubility. What binds a marriage together is rather (as the eastern churches have always insisted) the devoted and self-sacrificial fidelity of the spouses, a bond which may become solid at different stages of married life. If it fails to do so at all, it is at least arguable that the bond may never have existed and that it may be God's will to bring it into effect with a different partner.

Pastoral Considerations

It is probably fair to say, however, that this is not the level at which the question torments the conscience of many clergy and lay people today, whose reluctance to concede the possibility of remarriage after divorce proceeds not so much from the highly theoretical (and problematical) doctrine of indissolubility as from an obstinate sense of allegiance to that abhorrence of divorce so clearly expressed by Jesus. As we saw at the beginning, this is one matter on which there is no shadow of doubt: Jesus was (unlike the great majority of his contemporaries) utterly opposed to divorce, and the one way in which the community of his followers can effectively witness to this conviction is by repudiating the option of divorce for themselves. The merit of this approach is that it gives a clear message to the world that marriage, in the Christian understanding, is a lifelong commitment terminable only by death, and moreover it is manifestly faithful to the spirit of Jesus' teaching even if, in the letter of it, certain texts suggest at least the possibility of a more nuanced pastoral policy.

The problem arises, of course, when members of the community fail in their own marriages to achieve a lifelong loving relationship or when they yield to the temptation, at times (it seems) virtually overwhelming, of an adulterous union. The logic of the absolutist position seems to require that they should be expelled from the fellowship of the Church; but this is clearly incompatible with a gospel which has at its very heart the proposition that *no* sin (other than that against the Holy Spirit) is beyond the forgiveness of God. Moreover, if they have to leave the Church, where else can they go for the salvation of their souls?

Perhaps, then, they may be publicly disciplined, so that the standard of marriage demanded may be seen to be being upheld. But the only public penalty available is exclusion from the Eucharist. Until recently this was in fact imposed in the Church of England, as is still the case in the Roman Catholic Church, but even there it is being widely challenged, not merely on pastoral grounds (for how are sinful Christians to be nurtured if they are denied the means of grace?), but for theological reasons: the Eucharist is itself a sacrament of forgiveness and reconciliation, properly administered to those who have committed the most grievous sins so long as they are penitent. How then can exclusion from it be an appropriate consequence of the failure of a marriage? And in any case the Christian community itself may find it hard to see that a penal discipline is appropriate if the second union bears all the marks of a loving and lifelong commitment which were conspicuously absent from the first. This seems to leave only one possibility. If the offenders are to be allowed to remain in the congregation and to receive the sacraments, then at least they should not marry again. If either proposes to do so while the other is alive, he or she cannot expect the marriage to be publicly solemnized or acknowledged in church.

The strength of this policy is that it appears to give a clear message. The Church cannot prevent its members from falling into matrimonial disputes (though it may do everything possible to avert marriage breakdown). It recognizes that in certain cases divorce may be both the most prudent and the most humane course for the parties to take. It does not then expel them or deny them access to its sacramental life (which is now virtually the only form of worship in most parish churches). But if either contracts a second marriage while the other is alive this must be done elsewhere: it is something the Church cannot be seen to endorse by a public service. Moreover, if it does so it will seem to betray the faithfulness of those who in the past have shown obedience to ecclesiastical discipline by either renouncing the project of a second marriage or accepting the interdict on the second marriage taking place in a church. Thus the message remains clear and unambiguous. In obedience to the Lord's command (or rather, one version of it), it refuses to recognize a second marriage under these circumstances and so, by implication, condemns it.

It is, of course, precisely this implication which causes massive pastoral problems. If I have been divorced and have contracted a second marriage (as is the case for at least a quarter of married people today), how am I to be persuaded to join a church which explicitly and publicly condemns what I have done? If I do join, what sort of welcome may I expect from a congregation which has been taught that my present marriage is a breach of the standards expected of any member? Even if they show me sympathy and respect, shall I feel comfortable amid the prayers and praises of a community committed to avoiding and showing disapproval of the course I have taken myself? Shall I even welcome the visit of the parish priest whom I must regard as the representative of an institution which has shown its disapproval of my marriage by refusing to allow it to be solemnized in church?

It is the sheer pressure of such pastoral situations which has caused many clergy to believe that the 'clear message' on the lifelong and exclusive commitment involved in marriage is achieved at too high a price, and to take advantage of the discretion now available to them to conduct second marriages in their church. But the arguments that can be advanced against the absolutist policy are not merely pastoral. A matter of principle is involved.

We need to return to the point made at the very beginning, that there is no such thing as 'Christian marriage'. Marriage existed long before Christianity, and continues to exist quite independently of it. What Christianity (like other religions) does in respect of any particular marriage is invoke God's blessing on it, invite the prayers of the community to support it, and insist (with appropriate teaching and preparation) on the lifelong mutual commitment upon which the couple is entering. But the marriage itself – the statements of intent, the exchange of vows and of rings –

is a standard procedure wherever it takes place. There is no sense in which the Church can refuse to 'recognize' a marriage which takes place in a registry office; for the ceremony, in its essentials, is exactly the same wherever it happens. The only difference is that, in church, some prayers and devotional material are added; and if, as is often the case, a Christian minister performs a 'blessing' in church after the ceremony in a registry office, then the marriage is indistinguishable from one that is conducted in church throughout.

That a marriage is fully and properly performed so long as the formal requirements imposed by the State are observed was, as we have seen, the presupposition of all Christian thinking about marriage throughout the patristic and early medieval periods. There is nothing that the Church can add of material or legal import. If it refuses the hospitality of the church building, there is no sense in which it can claim that the marriage is inferior or deficient; and if it then provides a service of 'blessing' it is publicly conferring on the couple those opportunities for prayer, praise and Christian commitment which are the only unique and distinctive contribution which it makes to a wedding in the first place. The 'message' conveyed by an initial refusal is by no means so clear as it may have seemed at first sight; and the pastoral consequences for the Church's ministry and mission become ever more damaging as the divorce rate inexorably increases.

Conclusions

From this survey we may now draw certain conclusions which are of relevance to any discussion of the Church's discipline on marriage and divorce.

1. Marriage is a social institution of great antiquity, which the Christian Church, along with other religions, believes to be according to the will of God.

2. In Britain, as in many other countries, the essential elements of the marriage ceremony are the same whether or not it takes place in a church, and the couple is required to intend a lifelong commitment.

3. In antiquity, as in all contemporary societies not controlled or deeply influenced by the Roman Catholic Church (such as the Republic of Ireland) divorce was and is obtainable with varying degrees of ease or difficulty by legal process.

4. In Christianity, divorce is regarded not merely as a tragic disappointment of legitimate hopes and a serious risk to the upbringing of children but as a grave sin. To reflect Jesus' abhorrence of divorce his Church has always sought means to discourage its members from separation, divorce and remarriage

while the first partner is alive. These means have varied from absolute exclusion to mild disciplining, and have been tempered by the needs of a pastoral ministry towards those whose marriages have not prospered.

5. In no western culture (other than the medieval Church of the West) has it been maintained that marriage creates a bond which it is impossible to dissolve. The statement in Genesis that the two become 'one flesh' was never taken by Jewish or patristic interpreters to imply that a couple who were divorced were still somehow bound together. On the contrary, the whole purpose of the institution of divorce has been to release the parties from their marriage and make them free, if they so wish, to enter into another.

6. The only grounds on which it has been seriously argued that marriage creates a bond that is literally indissoluble are that marriage is a 'sacrament' and that the effects of a sacrament cannot be reversed or eliminated. This view was developed in the Western (though never in the Eastern) Church between the twelfth and fourteenth centuries and has determined the marriage discipline of the Roman Catholic Church ever since.

7. Sacramental indissolubility was rejected by the Protestant Churches as unscriptural and forms no part of the historic doctrine of the Church of England. Due, in part at least, to the influence of Anglo-Catholic theology in England towards the end of the nineteenth century it came to exercise a hold on

the teaching and practice of both the Church of England and the Anglican Communion which lasted for about half a century but is now widely questioned or abandoned.

8. In the absence of a doctrine of sacramental indissolubility, the considerations which must guide the Church in forming its marriage discipline are the same as have been present throughout its history. On the one hand it must show itself faithful to the teaching of Jesus which, though ambiguous in its practical application, expresses a consistent abhorrence of divorce. On the other hand it must continue to offer all its resources of healing and reconciliation to those whose marriages are brought to an end by forces they feel powerless to resist and who embark on a new marriage in a spirit of due penitence, faith and hope, and in the love which alone makes possible that union of man and wife which is an image and precious experience of the self-giving union of Christ and his Church.

Questions

Marriage: the Institution

1. What are the main reasons why people marry today? How are these different from the reasons people married in the past?

2. The Book of Genesis, endorsed by the Gospels, teaches that marriage was ordained by God. For much of its history, however, Israel was a polygamous society, in which a wife or wives were regarded as the property of a husband. To what extent is modern marriage the same institution as the one we read about in the Old Testament?

3. Read Matthew 19:10–12 and 1 Corinthians 7:25–38. How do you account for the different view taken of celibacy in Judaism and the New Testament? Does celibacy make any sense today?

4. What should be the Church's involvement with marriage? What do people really want from a church wedding?

Jesus and Divorce

1. Read Moses' teaching on divorce in Deuteronomy 24:1–4. Why did it lead to disputes about divorce, among the Jews in Jesus' time?

2. Compare Jesus' teaching about divorce and remarriage in Mark 10:2–9 and Matthew 19:3–9. What other differences are there in addition to the phrase 'except for adultery' in Matthew? Which version do you think is likelier to be the original?

3. The author argues that in his teaching against divorce Jesus himself was not laying down a new law, nor setting up an authoritarian discipline for the Church, but proclaiming an ideal moral standard with no hard and fast rules attached. Are you convinced?

4. If Matthew took Jesus' teaching on divorce to imply a rule for his community (as the author says he must have done), but then 'softened' it by adding the clause about adultery, what does that suggest about the kind of authority these verses should have for us today?

The Early Church

1. It appears, as the author notes, that the Church in general was soon forced to adapt Jesus' stance against divorce to the realities of community life. Does this seem to you wrong? Can you think of other instances of this kind of 'adaptation'?

2. What do you think of Athenagoras' view that marriage was not only for life, but for eternity? What is the biblical evidence against this view?

3. What do you understand by Jesus' words, 'What God has joined together, let no man put asunder'?

4. The author notes that in Ephesians 5:21-end, there is no reciprocity. The husband is urged to love and sacrifice himself for his wife as Christ loves and sacrifices himself for his body the Church; whereas the wife is urged to 'respect' or 'fear' her husband. (Contrast, however, 1 Corinthians 7:3,4 where husband and wife are said mutually to 'rule over' each other's bodies.) Do you think that the roles of husband and wife should be seen as totally equal and reciprocal, or is there a proper difference between them? If so, what is it?

St Augustine
1. What do you think the author of Ephesians 5 meant by comparing marriage to the relation between Christ and the Church? What does the comparison say to you?

2. Could you explain to someone how Augustine's reading of Ephesians 5 led him to believe that the married relationship was absolutely unbreakable? Why did it make a difference that Augustine did not know Greek, and so read Ephesians in Latin, not in the original?

Marriage as a Sacrament
1. What do you think are the necessary conditions for a marriage to be a true marriage? Do you think there is a difference between marriages which are cele-

brated with a church wedding and marriages which are not?

2. What do you understand by the word sacrament? Do you count marriage as being one or not?

3. Do you think there is a 'conjugal something' which makes a first marriage permanent? What happens to it if the marriage breaks up?

4. Do you think a couple are married before the marriage is sexually consummated? Or that an unmarried couple are in some sense married once they have sex?

5. Do you think 1 Corinthians 6:15–20 (which the author does not mention) may have a bearing on the argument?

Indissolubility
1. Explain how the description of marriage as a sacrament in the fullest technical sense leads to the belief that a true marriage must therefore be indissoluble.

2. Why, in Roman Catholic theology, can there really be no such thing as divorce, only nullity? What are the possible grounds, in such thinking, for proving nullity?

3. What might it mean to say that marriage is 'sacramental', but not in the same sense as the 'dominical' sacraments of baptism and the Eucharist?

4. Why does the author believe that the marriage teaching of the Eastern Orthodox Churches is closer to that of Ephesians 5?

5. Do you agree that the Western tradition has made a mistake by concentrating so much on the idea of the 'consummation' of marriage by the first act of intercourse?

The Church of England
1. How did Anglo-Catholicism influence the Church of England towards a harder line on divorce and remarriage earlier in this century?

2. Does it seem to you a satisfactory state of affairs that remarriage after divorce in the Church of England depends on the conscience of individual clergy? If not, how would you change the position?

3. The present rules of the Roman Catholic Church lay down that marriages conducted by Roman Catholic clergy are indissoluble, but those conducted outside are not. Can you see any virtue in this position?

4. The author's closing sentences seem to suggest an alternative form of nullity, based on discerning marriages where a 'bond of devoted and self-sacrificial fidelity' seems never to have come about. Might it be practically possible to build a marriage discipline on this idea? Would it cover the majority of divorces that now take place?

Pastoral Considerations

1. Do you think any form of Church discipline should be imposed on Christians who divorce? Or on Christians who remarry after divorce? If so, what?

2. What are the personal and pastoral problems involved in refusing second marriages in a church? What are the problems and risks involved in accepting them?

3. Does it make any theological sense to refuse second marriages in church but to bless them when they have taken place in a registry office?

4. When, if ever, should remarriage of a divorced person be allowed in church?

Conclusions

1. Have you changed your views as a result of reading this book?

2. How and why?